The Greatest Escape (In the History of Huddersfield Town F.C.)

by

J.B. Lockwood

Bloomington, IN   Milton Keynes, UK
authorHOUSE®

AuthorHouse™
1663 Liberty Drive, Suite 200
Bloomington, IN 47403
www.authorhouse.com
Phone: 1-800-839-8640

AuthorHouse™ UK Ltd.
500 Avebury Boulevard
Central Milton Keynes, MK9 2BE
www.authorhouse.co.uk
Phone: 08001974150

© 2007 J.B. Lockwood. All rights reserved.

No part of this book may be reproduced, stored in a retrieval system, or transmitted by any means without the written permission of the author.

First published by AuthorHouse 6/12/2007

ISBN: 978-1-4259-9678-9 (sc)

Printed in the United States of America
Bloomington, Indiana

This book is printed on acid-free paper.

An Introductory Word from the Author.

I remember so clearly the times I used to wait for the Cowshed gates to open at the old Leeds Road at the half-time interval. A restless group would wait for the gateman to give the sign that he was ready to let the noisy army through before anyone was hurt; hence a wave of excited fans would rush past the ever present official to add to the atmosphere that was already present in the shed.

We knew that permission to join the others was not in doubt. What we did not know, however, was who would be the 'talk of the Town' after the game. Ones such as Denis Law, Ray Wilson and Frank Worthington must have had burning ears over the years, not to mention the likes of Alan Gowling, Steve Kindon, Andy Booth and Malcolm Brown. These are just a small minority of those who were unable to escape the public's eyes and ears over the years.

Despite a painful move to the Galpharm Stadium, nothing has changed in this regard; there has usually been someone who has grabbed the headlines; Marcus Stewart will tell you that the 'talk of the Town' label sill stuck long after the sad farewell to the former ground.

However, since the Greatest Escape in the history of the club, to me, there has been a vital change of emphasis. That is, no matter who captures the attention on the field, I cannot ignore the life- saving efforts of it. Obviously, enormous credit rightly belongs to Ken Davy and those that stuck by him during the darkest hours; ones such as Terry Fisher and Martyn Byrne readily come to mind. Having said this, the ones who were there to pick up the wreckage in the aftermath of relegation should always be remembered in conversation. The Survival Trust, along with the 517 bondholders, to me, should always have a special place in Town folklore as well as the thousands of fans who helped keep the club afloat.

Therefore, whoever gains the most praise on the field in the years to come should never draw attention away from the huge commitment of those off the pitch who should always be 'the talk of the Town..

Chapter 1: Vale of Tears

5-1.That was the disastrous, miserable, heartbreaking score at Port Vale which condemned Town to relegation in the 2002-03 season.

This ample conformation that we would be playing football once more in the basement division was accompanied by tears. Whether you had decided to leave early or stay until the bitter end (and it was bitter) there was no hiding from the shattering blow and the feeling of surrender. The football had not flowed but the tears certainly had at Vale Park. It was a cruel irony of how the fixtures turned out that we needed to beat the side that always seemed to have the mastery over us in order to have any chance of survival. If there was one team that I would have wanted to avoid with so much at stake it would have been Port Vale. I would not have fancied our chances at home let alone away. Hence I should not have been surprised to see everything falling apart on the field, as Vale ran away with the game.

These were not tears of joy as some may have experienced after the famous Great Escape but those of despair.

The Greatest Escape (In the History of Huddersfield Town F.C.)

It was not just the thought of being trapped in the lowest division that left many stunned, but the increasing awareness that our very survival was at stake; this was hard to veil at Vale Park.

It was in the midst of this heartbreaking scenario that I remember being one of the very last ones left in the ground with three fans. One of these, Mark Ainley, I had known for many years whereas the other two I had never met in my life. This however, did not stop Mark, I and another female supporter along with her daughter having a hug as we were united in grief. Mark Ainley known by many as a leader of the fans was still taking the lead by trying to comfort the Mum and daughter, as he himself was visibly moved by the occasion. We simply could not hide the sheer disappointment that was all around, nor could we veil the enormity of the crisis that threatened to wipe out the famous blue and white outfit.

The mother of the child had composed a poem about the Terriers. This was a noble attempt to help the Survival Trust which had been formed out of desperation. The poem, which she read to us all, was her contribution in trying to lift the spirits, to raise awareness of the desperate plight of the club, to send out a rallying call to the troops of Huddersfield Town. Her poetic inspiration was her way of fighting the blackest period in the history of the club, having been within eight days from closure before the Trust was formed. It was her way of playing for time for the club, in contrast to the players at Vale Park; I am sure that they could not wait for the game to end, to get off the field, to hear the final whistle blow. However, it was another whistle that we were dreading that would signal the end of the club that we were so keen to avoid, to put it mildly.

As a matter of interest, Robbie Williams had just brought out a new album called Escapology. On the front cover he was hanging upside down with a rope tied around his legs. However, Port Vale's favourite Son did not look in any distress; in fact he gave the impression that he could wriggle to safety at any time. This was in contrast to the blue and white outfit which was well and truly trapped and facing the handicap of relegation once more to add to financial woes that no one could disguise. Instead of the rope being tied around the feet, however, as in the former Take That star, it was a symbolic noose that was ever tightening around the neck of the club. The fact that six players had been booked seemed a trivial statistic as we barely contemplated facing Oldham Athletic in our last game with and with nothing at stake apart from the issue of the future of the Terriers.

The Jason Gavin goal was scant consolation in view of the subsequent collapse that was to follow. He was with us for a short spell on loan and it was nice to see him on the score sheet, but the kind of loan that was required to ensure the greatest escape in the history of the club was somewhere in the region of around £20m; in fact, even if all the players had been sold, there would still have been no chance of clearing the massive debt. We had witnessed the Great Escape in the 1997-98 season which had been captured on video by my old school friend, when Town clawed their way to safety against the odds. I can imagine this giving way to tears of joy for some, but these were tears of sheer misery. The anguish was evident amongst distressed supporters not only because we had just been relegated, but due to the fact that they did not know if there would be another season left for the Blues.

As we witnessed the Port Vale fans without a care in the world the same could not be said about the troubled Town fans who were feeling blue for the wrong reason. The home fans were slowly making their way home in the comforting knowledge that they were totally safe for another season; the same could not be said about those who had made the journey from Yorkshire. The unthinkable was not only possible, but it was looking ever more likely that the club would have to fold. This began to dominate our thoughts especially after witnessing the surrender of the team which would continue to gnaw away at us for much longer than just the journey home.

Chapter 2: S.O.S.

It was at this particular time that Britain and America were at war with Iraq. Sadly, many people were caught up in the conflict resulting in a heavy loss of lives. The S.O.S. (Save Our Souls) as regards the ones who were in dire straits had fallen on deaf ears for some as they were caught up in the crossfire. Those who were in a position to surrender found a measure of relief from the heavy artillery, yet their escape from this would be at a price as they faced the hardship of imprisonment; true freedom would only come at the end of the war itself. Yet despite this desperate situation there were some light hearted moments which are worthy of consideration amidst the depression of the prolonged onslaught. As a matter of fact there was one person who unwittingly gave me inspiration and a measure of comfort in the wake of Town's relegation.

This particular figure who caught the attention of everyone was the Iraqi foreign information minister who had been nicknamed Comical Ali. He had been so named due to his comical, outrageous comments in the face of inevitable defeat. In fact, even as the tanks were closing in on the Iraqi soldiers who were taking the last stand against the enemy, his unflinching manner was a source of much amusement as he was being interviewed, by a British reporter.

However, it was not only his utter calmness against overwhelming odds that gave him his charm, but the fact that he took the lead in trying to instill coolness in others. Hence, he was an ideal candidate in helping me to attempt to lift the misery that the proud club was experiencing. Thus I tried to use his example to bring a measure of relief to the community. I did this by making known that I was drawing a picture of the man of the moment in his beret and spectacles, albeit in the famous blue and white.

I recall the instance when he was being interviewed by a reporter, taking careful note of what he had said. When asked if he was afraid whilst being surrounded by tanks and gunfire, he replied, "No, and don't you be afraid." This seemed even more amusing if you take into account that the reporter was British! Thus, I adapted his mentality to fit the agonizing circumstances that the Terriers found themselves in. Hence, in my version he was asked if he was sad in the aftermath of Town's relegation. His predictable reply was, "No, and don't you be sad, the Town are staying up!" The fact that I had drawn him in blue and white with the Mc Alpine stadium in the background gave the picture more impact. It was my way of easing the tension that everyone was experiencing as I attempted to raise awareness of the desperate plight that the club was facing, at one stage being only eight days from closure.

COMICAL ALI

Therefore, the message was not in a bottle as is usually the case in sending out an S.O.S. but on paper, as I did what I could to remind the public of the sad struggle that we were all facing.

The club was all at sea with no real hope on the horizon. We were just about keeping afloat due to the passion and commitment of the fans who could not imagine life without the boys in blue and white. It is true that in the Great Escape that Jacko and Terry Yorath masterminded, safety from relegation was a result of efforts from players on the field, whereas the battle was now confined to the efforts off it. In other words if the Greatest Escape was going to be realized it would have to come about without so much as kicking a ball. This is why there was such an S.O.S (SAVE OUR SIDE) call from the fans who knew that the club was in deep water; in fact we were drowning in debt. We needed loyal fans such as Mark Ainley, Andy Morris, Gassy, Bruce, Bluey and Knighty to help our plight to safety. I felt sure that we could rely on ones like Harry Webster, Irish, Batesy, Knoppy, Donna and Tony and Paul Callaghan. I never did find out why these two brothers were called GPO 1 and GPO 2 but all that mattered now was that we could call on such ones to deliver the goods for the club.

I suppose when your team is on the brink of closure the memories come flooding back; the ups and downs, the highs and lows. I thought about the times that I had shared with my old school friend Simon Normington who has successfully made many videos for Huddersfield Town, the most famous, being the Great Escape. This had documented the remarkable recovery from the very brink of relegation when the side was well adrift at the foot of the table; yet they still made it to 'dry land.'

Having said this, there was one occasion when he captured me on film many years ago when I turned my back on Town. What do I mean by this? Well on one glorious occasion at the Valley, Simon had somehow taken a video shot of me jumping wildly up and down after Steve Kindon had scored his second goal of the match, to put Town 2-1 up. Out of sheer delight you could only see the back of me as I 'lost it' for a few moments as I found myself again amidst a sea of blue and white fans. We both played the tape back to our amusement as we witnessed the goals from big Steve. He not only saved our side on that unforgettable day, but also showed how to wrap up the points in style.

Thus, I admit that I turned my back on the Terriers, but it was for the right reason. Having travelled all the way to London to see my beloved club was an evidence of my passionate loyalty for which I was well rewarded with punishing strikes from Kindo. I never turned my back on Huddersfield Town then, in the wrong kind of way, and I certainly had no intention of abandoning the blue and white outfit when they needed me most.

However, there was one instance when Simon and I were not together when I experienced that S.O.S. feeling. But instead of the letters standing for 'save our souls' or 'save our side,' for me it came to stand for Southend- on- Sea. I recall being only 14 when I made the long trip to the coast with no idea as to the sinking, trapped feeling that I would experience before my return.

On arriving at the ground after a long journey to see my beloved team, there was no indication as to how the hatred and rivalry would erupt into ugly scenes on the terraces.

The Terriers had got off to a bright start and were coasting on the coast when trouble erupted. To my adolescent horror, I found myself surrounded by the home fans that were making life difficult for us. Suddenly and without warning there was a blue and white rush to get to safety, to scramble on to the pitch. Instinctively, I had to make the decision whether or not to follow the rest in the dash for the wall as I saw some being helped on to the pitch. A captain may be renowned for staying until the bitter end but I simply panicked and tried to follow the rest. However, when I realised that I was not going to make it to safety, in a split second, I put on a pretense of being one of the Southend fans who were chasing the Town supporters on to the pitch. This I did by pointing and shouting at my own supporters in an attempt to save my skin. When I swayed back with the home fans I can't describe the sheer terror that I felt that I might have been exposed as away supporter. Having said this, it is surprising how convincing you can be at acting when you are frightened to death. Without the comforting sight of such ones as Ged, Pete Lyons, Billy Barraclough, Basher Bennett(R.I.P.)Stavo and Chris Sunderland (R.I.P.) I had to act out of sheer desperation. The overwhelming sense of anxiety was hardly relieved by words of comfort from someone standing next to me. This was someone that had taken me to the pub before the game and who was trying to offer reassurance that I would be safe so long as I stood by him. However, the fact that I had only met him before the game probably went some way to explaining why I was still terrified without the likes of Patty, Tatty, Ronnie Shaw and Woody. Having said this, I am grateful to this West Ham fan who was visiting the match that he did not betray this fourteen year old with a Yorkshire accent.

However, I did manage to tunnel myself to safety after nervously testing the waters. This I did by measuring the reactions on the faces of those around me, before slipping away to relative safety, but since I was still in the wrong end, I would have much rather have preferred to be safe with a relative!

All things considered, it is true to say that I did not have a chance to send out an S.O.S; I was simply relieved to keep my disguise intact, as I eventually made my great escape out of the ground despite further waves of violence.

Returning to the present day, however, the safety of Huddersfield Town was far from secure; in fact they were well out of their depth, and on the verge of experiencing financial shipwreck. There was no option but to send out an S.O.S. to the public. In fact, it was not possible to hide the fact that the club was in a mess. The bucket collections simply stressed the need for at least a temporary lifeline to keep the Blues afloat.

In the case of the Great Escape the tunnel to security was dependent on results on the field. In other words the players had their destiny in their own hands to some extent. By simply winning games and picking up enough points survival was guaranteed, whereas in this scenario there was no guarantee whatsoever of an escape route unless around £20 million was going to be raised which seemed highly unlikely. The ship was far from steady and it was going to take a monumental effort to stop it capsizing altogether. This is why it would be the Greatest Escape of all time as far as the Terriers were concerned.

However, despite the bucket collections being a drop in the ocean, it demonstrated the desire, passion and commitment of the fans. This would have to be in greater measure and more sustained than the one

The Greatest Escape (In the History of Huddersfield Town F.C.)

masterminded by Jacko and the team of the late nineties if we were to swim to safety. There had to be an even greater focus from everyone involved to eclipse the successful outcome of the massive relegation battle of the past, one which had been so well documented by my old friend Simon Normington. The closest thing that we had to an anchor was the Survival Trust which was giving a measure of leadership and direction but there was no hint of surrender as we gratefully accepted the lifeline from the other clubs. The S.O.S. was being sent out to everyone in the Football League and almost every club contributed to the financial crisis, putting aside feelings of rivalry and competitiveness, to their credit. Having said this, although the financial gestures were appreciated from all, which stemmed the tide somewhat, there was no escaping the fact we were stranded and on the verge of drowning in debt. Despite this, however, no one showed any desire to abandon the ship. Having said this, it was safe to say that if we were going to turn things around and go from one ASBO (a sorry blue outfit) to another ASBO (a safe blue outfit) then we had to weather the storms of uncertainty and unforeseen difficulties if we were to have any chance of making it safely to shore. Find out in the next chapter how I tackled one of these areas of uncertainty in an attempt to help edge us ever so slightly towards survival.

Chapter 3: Thin Blue Line.

The expression thin blue line usually refers to the police; it is used in the context of when their resources are stretched to breaking point. Although I would like to mention the valuable contribution of the constabulary in helping the blue and white outfit, it is the thin blue line of the team that more readily comes to mind. This line was thinner than any that I had known in the history Huddersfield Town; in fact, it was so lean that the police themselves offered their services to contribute to the much needed relief for the football club; this they did by apparently not demanding the full amount of pay for their workload on some occasions. It highlighted the desperate situation that the club was in. We were on the right side of the law; hence the much appreciated help on the part of the force. We were, however, on the wrong side of the creditors including the Inland Revenue. Having said this, the possibility of the Greatest Escape was still as unlikely as ever, but extended time from the Inland Revenue helped to give a continued flicker of hope. The persistent efforts and negotiations of the hard working M.P. Barry Sheerman in this regard gave everyone a measure of relief as more time was given to the club. We were playing for time but there was no time for play. In the well documented Great Escape by my old school friend Simon Normington, the referee's whistle was all important. Now, however, it was the fear of the creditors blowing the whistle on the club that was the biggest fear. With the Great Escape the official's whistle could be a source of relief or disappointment depending on the result at the time. The blowing of the creditor's whistle, however, could only mean one thing; the end of the hope of any Greatest Escape for Huddersfield Town.

However, before I mention the scenario in more detail, I would like to briefly roll back the years to when I was still at school and I experienced a thin blue line of a different nature.

My friend Simon must have wished he had been with me when I decided to have a day off school to see the Town play at Torquay one Wednesday evening.

Apparently, my absence in the classroom was duly noted when the Headmaster asked the class if they knew where I was. On receiving blank looks, he openly told them he had an idea as to where I might be. Despite receiving no helpful information as to my whereabouts, he nevertheless came back into the classroom with a fixture list in an attempt to confirm his suspicions. But could he really believe that I would go all the way to the south coast to see my team in midweek action? I think he could!

The thin blue line was evident that evening on the south coast as only one coach turned up to make up the away support. Moreover, the match was quite forgettable as we lost 2-1 which edged us further towards the wrong end of the table. However, I doubt whether the Head would forget that I was not in attendance when he came into the classroom. The only table that I should have been concerned with was the one provided for me in the school classroom, and not where my team was in the League.

When I returned the next morning one of my friends told me that I get away with murder as he went on to tell me about the enquiry into my whereabouts. The fact that the Headmaster had decided to draw a line under my going astray convinced me that perhaps he was right; on reflection it was a case of getting away with blue murder! My midweek madness had gone unpunished even though my team could not reward me with a result!

However, despite the unrewarding experience of going all the way to see my team lose on the south coast, I knew that I would still have a team to follow on my return. Although I had ample time to reflect on the missed opportunities on the coach after the match I knew that there would be more chances to put matters right on the field. This was in sharp contrast to the events that were now taking place at the Galpharm Stadium. With a good night's sleep and a decent excuse for my being absent from school I could soon get over the defeat at Plainmoor(home of Torquay United) How, though, do you deal with the fact that your team is on the brink of oblivion and that there may not even be a starting line-up the following season? No matter how bitterly disappointed we may have been in the past, there had always been a chance of putting things right; this was true even in the face of successive relegations

The Greatest Escape (In the History of Huddersfield Town F.C.)

in the absence of a Great Escape. However, now we found ourselves in a scenario where the players were not in charge as the fans clung to only a small measure of control that could soon be evaporated at any time. Having said this, we had to hold on to any grip that we had of the situation. Find out how I personally tried to reduce the overwhelming odds to save the Blues from going into a financial black hole.

Chapter 4: Reach for the stars

The expression 'reaching for the stars' can be translated as trying to be as positive as is possible. You can reach for the stars in a literal sense (although it would be hopeless even in a rocket) or in another sense which is more appropriate to the survival quest which had already begun. It was far easier to reach for the bars, and I do not criticize anybody that did this to ease the stress, but there would always be a pub around; the same could not be said about the blue and white regime. When the pubs call time they are only closed until the following day, whereas closing time with the Terriers would mean a permanent hangover.

Hence, if the proud Yorkshire outfit was going to rekindle the cosmic feelings of the past then it called for an unstoppable spirit in order to survive. The club which can boast of many quality players like Denis Law, Frank Worthington and Ray Wilson should not go down without a fight. Although there was plenty of debris from the aftermath of relegation, I hope I speak for all when I say that it was unthinkable that we should surrender our proud heritage without a struggle; one

The Greatest Escape (In the History of Huddersfield Town F.C.)

that would surpass that found in the Great Escape. A campaign had been launched in the minds and hearts of the fans that was slowly gaining momentum in raising an awareness of our desperate situation.

I mentioned earlier my friend Simon Normington with whom I shared many happy memories which go all the way back to early childhood. His outside involvement with the club has become well known due to making of many videos about the Terriers. Little did he know what influence this contribution would have on me later in my life, although I should have known that he would make an impact somewhere along the way.

I recall on one occasion when Simon reached for the stars in a somewhat different sense when we were much younger. Perhaps it would be more accurate to say that he was waiting for the stars. We had both been to see Town play Millwall at Leeds Road and we had lost the game by a controversial decision. However, after the match Simon had waited for the stars, which were the Millwall team to get on the bus. What followed next left me shocked as I saw my friend get on the coach to protest about the unfair decision with passion to the entire Millwall team bus. Having been encouraged to leave the coach with no harm done, I couldn't help feeling that he himself had had a great escape of his own.

It was this kind of passion for the club that was needed to build on the delicate platform that we had already established. It was this kind of spirit, if channeled in the right way that would help the club to defy financial gravity.

Hence, I tried to help promote an explosive spirit to blast away the cobwebs of depression that were hovering over the club. This I did by co-operating with the Survival Trust as I offered my services as an artist. Having said this it took the word a while to spread around the ground. I remember being approached by security from the adjoining section of the stadium that was suspicious of my intentions. The subdued look on my face after the confirmation of relegation at the weekend was not enough to convince him that I was a fan; he needed assurance of my commitment to the club. Hence on the miserable Monday morning after returning from Port Vale, he approached me as though I had never been to a game in my life. As I slowly convinced him that my intentions were good he left me staring at the empty ground which did nothing to ease my obvious sadness.

Putting these feelings aside, however, in order to fuel the positive spirit that was emerging, I put myself on show at the ground as I decided to paint the Mc Alpine Stadium (now known as the Galpharm Stadium.) It was no time to hide, but rather to stand up and be counted. As it turned out, I sat down to be counted as I set up my chair in order to capture the stadium as an artist. This was a good way to raise the profile of the financial crisis that we were facing as I was in a good position to answer any questions that anyone chose to ask. In, fact, rather keeping a low profile, I chose the most conspicuous place that I could think of, even on a match day; a place where I was clearly visible to clusters of fans. This way I was able to remind the supporters that I was making prints available to the public.

ME AT THE McALPINE STADIUM (NOW THE GALPHARM)

In the past, the remarkable recovery that saved the Blues from relegation was restricted to what happened on the field, whereas in this instance any massive turnaround depended on activities solely off the pitch. Hence, I had to give it my best shot without kicking a ball.

As an artist I wanted to shine as brightly as I possibly could in helping the cause; this was my way of reaching for the stars. However, although I hoped that this would radiate enthusiasm to others, in attempting to accomplish the survival mission, I felt it was necessary to reach for the stars in a different sense. In order to add fuel to the fire I decided to approach the players at the club, ones such as Andy Booth, David Mirfin, and Rob Edwards amongst others. I did not ask them for any money, since I figured that if they signed the prints it would add to their value.

ME AND ANDY BOOTH

Hence, with no persuasion on my part the players and former stars such as Kieran O' Regan, Chris Lucketti and Tom Cowan kept things moving for the cause. Therefore, by reaching for the stars in a new sense, I certainly was not abandoning my positive attitude, in fact I was adding to it.

KIERAN O' REGAN

Above all, there was no sign of anyone giving up on the future of Huddersfield Town having a team of shooting stars for the next season. However, in order to give more added weight to our survival mission I felt the need to extend the invitation to others outside the club. The fact that Jacko and Terry Yorath had contributed with their signatures without hesitation, was evidence of their continued passion and desire to help the Terriers. However, I certainly did not feel that it was a negative move on my part to involve other big names or even legends where possible. I knew that Peter and Terry would be remembered for a long time to come for their part in the remarkable recovery of the past, but this time the outcome was no longer restricted to results on the field as I mentioned earlier.

Thus, who could I persuade to come on board to help bring about the biggest turnaround that the club had ever known? Who would give their support in raising awareness for the plight, the fight and the right for the Terriers to remain as a football team? This question will be answered in the next chapter as I got in touch with two legends of the game.

Chapter 5: Missing Links

This expression is usually found in the singular rather than in the plural. When you hear the phrase missing link it conjures up ideas of an evolutionary chain; the missing connection between man and ape. However, since I was trying to link big names with the club, then there had to be more than one. My search had nothing to do with apes or monkeys although at times I did feel I had to be a bit cheeky!

Therefore, I had to figure out who was or had been connected with the club; someone with charisma or who had commanded respect in the game. Up until now I had only approached the ones with a strong link to the Terriers, but now it was time to look beyond the present day outfit.

Therefore, who could I turn to in order to help to further raise the spirit of the famous Yorkshire outfit?

On reflection, I decided to write to someone called Carol Washington at Nottingham Forest who had been a fan of Huddersfield Town for many years. By so doing, I was hoping to find a way through to the legendary Brian Clough, since she had been his secretary for a

The Greatest Escape (In the History of Huddersfield Town F.C.)

number of years at the City ground. I figured that there would be more chance of securing Cloughie's signature by approaching his former secretary than by any other method. I recall the occasion of Cloughie's retirement and the fond farewell that he publicly paid to Carol after her valuable years of service. I can understand if she felt a little shy when he put his arm around her and simply said something like "Beauty. Come here Beauty," as he managed to hold back the tears. This is what I did as I waited for a response from the man who had won the European Cup twice with Forest in successive seasons. We needed a charismatic influence or someone with leadership to be involved with the club in any way possible. I thought that if nothing else, he might join in our ultimate survival campaign if only for Carol's sake. Hence, it was only a weak link, but it could lead to a strong message being sent out to the football world if Brian chose to sign my prints.

Continuing to work along with the Survival Trust, I then decided to write to Sir Bobby Robson. Here again, the connection was far from obvious. I forged a link with the former England manager and the club only after careful consideration. It was not actually an attachment that he had with the Town; I had very little at my disposal. What I did remind him of however, was the fact that he that he had reputedly recommended the former manager Mick Wadswoth, but things had not worked out as anticipated. Hence, rather than dwelling on the past, I asked him if he could help in a small way at least save our future. This request was accompanied by four of my prints of the ground. I asked him to sign three of them which would be for sale immediately, and I also sent one for himself. It was my way of saying that there were no hard feelings about how matters had worked out on the field if he had put Mick forward as manager. Not only that, but when we needed all the help that we could get, I thought it was a fitting gesture under the circumstances. The association of Sir Bobby's name with the Blues was a weak one, but nonetheless by appealing to his good nature there was a chance that I could turn this avenue into a strong advert for us. I had begun my journey without a compass, but if I could secure Sir Bobby's signature it would help me to get on the map as regards further recruits.

BOBBY ROBSON

Therefore, as I waited for replies from two giants of the game my efforts were nonetheless still dwarfed by the enormous size of the debt that was still outstanding.

The Greatest Escape (In the History of Huddersfield Town F.C.)

The club was in administration as everybody took each day at a time, as we all tried to edge the club a little nearer to survival. I could sum the feelings up in one way by saying that we wanted someone to take the blues away without taking away the Blues!

Thus with time still against us I decided it struck me that there was someone else who had an attachment to someone who had had a bond with the club. This was none other than Kevin Keegan. How though did I arrive at this conclusion? The living legend has been associated with clubs like Liverpool, Newcastle, Southampton and Hamburg, but not with Huddersfield Town. He has even managed England after successful spells with Newcastle and Fulham but he has never been known to have a fondness for the Terriers.

However, it is no secret that Kevin has had such a wonderful history with Bill Shankly who made an impression at Leeds Road in his early days. Like Sir Bobby he has no direct attachment to the blue and white outfit but he played some marvelous, captivating football under someone who had a blue bond, namely Bill Shankly.

Hence, I felt that I had a genuine appeal for Kevin's help, as I reminded him of the honours that he won with his time at Liverpool. In writing to the former England star, I was keen to remind him of the contribution that Shanks had made to the heritage of the club. I did not want the breathtaking reality to escape his notice that the Terriers were on the brink of bankruptcy. Moreover, I felt the need to spell out just how upset Bill Shankly would have been to see the club with such a proud tradition slip away. Hence, without feeling intrusive,

I asked Kevin to sign my prints in memory of the late legend. It is hard to imagine that someone as genuine as Kevin Keegan would dismiss this request without careful thought, but to make an even greater impact on him I made the letter more interesting. I told him that he was not only my boyhood hero, but that if he signed my prints to help in the Greatest Escape then I would be thrilled; in fact, sensing the confidence whist writing the letter, I said that I would love it; I would really really love it. The reference to his reply to Sir Alex Ferguson I hoped would no doubt be apparent in my request. Thus in trying to 'hit the spot' to secure his signature I felt pleased with my efforts in making my feelings known, not just for me but for the struggling men in blue and white. By releasing my true feelings to Kevin, I was definitely not false to the club of my youth who were still trapped in dire circumstances.

Hence, I sent the letters to the legends in the midst of ongoing bucket collections organized by the Survival Trust. My friend Simon Normington had excelled in making the video the Great Escape for the club, finding inspiration from the War film which was full of plotting and camouflage. However, there was no disguising the desperate situation as the collections persisted, not incognito, but in full view of everybody. We still had the wrong kind of ASBO hanging over our heads, but would the return of the 'Prodigal Son' help turn A SORRY BLUE OUTFIT into a SAFE one. Find out in the next chapter as the identity of this one is revealed.

Chapter 6: The Return of the Prodigal Son?

In the parable of the prodigal son the person leaves home after receiving his inheritance form his father. In the course of time, he squandered his money on a lavish lifestyle. It is only when penniless that he finally comes to his senses and wishes to return home. Before going any further there was someone who fit the description of a son leaving home and had a desire to return to help the cause. However, it was not this one that was penniless, but rather the club that was practically broke. Hence, when Frank Worthington decided that he would return to the place where he first made his mark it could be said that it was a kind of homecoming. The fact that he was willing to show his support to the club in a charity game would not only give the Terriers a financial boost, but would give the fans a chance to welcome him back.

The Greatest Escape (In the History of Huddersfield Town F.C.)

However, when the ace decided to raise funds by playing for one of the star-studded teams it could only mean that it would help the positive spirit that was already in evidence; this could only help in providing an escape route.

Hence, Frank was like the prodigal son in the sense that he left his 'home' which included many happy memories for Huddersfield Town at Leeds Road to return once more. The Son in the parable had no choice but to throw himself at his Father's mercy on his return whereas the former Golden Boot winner had choice in the matter; in fact it could be said that Frank's homecoming was a complete contrast to that of the Son in the sense that it was the club that was in desperation rather than the ex- England star. For the club to find a way out of the biggest crisis ever, it needed people like Frank Worthington to continue to raise money and the profile of the enormous struggle ahead.

GOLDEN BOOT

ME AND FRANK

Another contrast between the two sons is that involving the reception that was anticipated by the homecoming. Whereas in the historical account the Son is anxious as to what his Father will think about the fortune that he has squandered, whereas Frank would surely have no such reservations and uncertainty; in fact I am sure that he could not wait to hear the welcome roar that would soon be heard on his behalf. The fact that he was given a testimonial at Leeds Road confirmed how highly the fans held him in esteem during his playing days. Whereas the Prodigal Son in the parable was ashamed to face his Father, no doubt the Shelf born star was full of pride to be chosen to return for such a worthy cause; there was no doubt that the fans appreciated his help in the mercy mission.

Thus the big man played his part in the game the All Stars and the Wembley Wizards; he even managed to get to half-time!

The Greatest Escape (In the History of Huddersfield Town F.C.)

There were many big names who contributed to the enjoyable spectacle but it seemed to me that it was the wonder of Worthy that still had the crowd in the most delightful admiration; hence the rapturous applause when he left the field.

I hope that I have not exhausted the comparison between Frank and the Son in the parable that has come down to us today, since I want to conclude on a happy, joyous note for both parties.

The conclusion of the son's return was one of joyous relief as his Father threw himself upon him and tenderly kissed his neck time and again, and stressed the point that this was his son who was dead but who had now come back to life. The homecoming scenario involving the former England ace was very similar. The fans were overjoyed to see him and carried this intensity over into the post match gathering where it was difficult to approach him without being in the way of autograph hunters. However, Frank to his credit was very patient with the well behaved fans that had come along to get a glimpse of their hero as was his partner Carol who was not complaining at having to share him for the day. Hence, the charity match had raised badly needed funds in order to help the club. Moreover, the fans, I am sure appreciated the efforts of all the former players who took part in the game that attracted thousands. However, although the money was a lifeline, there was still a long way to go before we would have any chance of saying that the club which was as good as dead had now come back to life

Chapter 7: Italian Job Well Done.

The financial situation seemed to becoming more complicated with no end in sight. It was a scrappy scenario involving the creditors and deadlines to be met, and was made even more complicated by trying to find someone who was willing to take on the club for the right price before time ran out.

However, despite the lingering uncertainty that was associated with the club I received a definite boost when Sir Bobby Robson sent back signed copies of my prints which were to go on general sale. Despite the entangled web of debt it was nice to see signatures from the former England manager as clear evidence of his backing for the blue and white army. We may have been without a manager ourselves but it was nice to see the Newcastle boss waste no time in showing his support for the proud Yorkshire outfit.

My persistence in behalf of the Terriers was further rewarded when the man in charge of the Manchester City job also replied to me with signatures that would be put to good use. Again the clear indication of support from Kevin Keegan, another former England manager, was a

The Greatest Escape (In the History of Huddersfield Town F.C.)

really helpful way of reminding people of the crisis that the club was in; not only that but it showed that if the club folded it would make a difference not just to the fans but also to high profile names in the world of football.

Hence, being spurred on by the encouraging replies in behalf of the Town, I decided that there was a job to be done that involved more than simply writing letters.

Therefore, I decided that I would go on a reconnaissance mission to the European Cup Final at Old Trafford where A.C.Milan were about to take on Juventus for the major honours in club football.

The fact that I did not have a ticket did not hold me back from showing an adventurous spirit. Hence, eager to avoid the despair of failure, I made up my mind to join the party atmosphere of the most two most successful sides in Europe for the season in question. I was on my way to the Theatre of Dreams as I was fully awake to the possibility of adding more signatures to my collection. I was not concerned about seeing the cream of Italian football but rather I was keenly aware of the big names that this fixture would attract. I was happy to travel without a ticket since it was not the result on the pitch that mattered but once again it was the result off the field that was the most important factor on this balmy evening. It may have been approaching summer, on this ideal venue for the Final, but it was still a wintry outlook back at the Galpharm as I was determined to bring further rays of hope.

The atmosphere at Old Trafford with that back at the McAlpine Stadium was very evident. I felt like an uninvited guest to the Italian party that was well under way by the time that I arrived on the scene in

J.B. Lockwood

Manchester. The carnival spirit was in striking contrast to the anxiety and uncertainty at the Mc Alpine that was threatening to overwhelm the positive outlook that had been built up over the last few months.

However, I had to try to continue to search out ways to help the club along with many more that had joined in the rescue package. I had to keep up the efforts to try and put the brakes on the downwards spiral that the club was still experiencing. I was surrounded by banners, flags and noisy horns, but the noisiest bells in my mind were still the ones that were continuing to ring out for the future of Huddersfield Town.

Hence, even if I never saw any of the match, I still had the opportunity to meet high profile people who could sign my work which would add value to it. I could not allow the casual party atmosphere to hinder my commitment and purpose to the Blues who were skidding around in a financial sense. I did not want the highly relaxed setting to weaken my resolve in helping my club out of danger.

Thus, having kept my focus in this regard, it was not long before I felt that I was in the driving seat as I quickly approached Roy Keane. The only indication as to his presence was the excited cries from some Manchester United fans that were as keen as me to secure his autograph. As he signed the print of the McAlpine I asked him if he had ever heard of goldenbrush. Despite the smile on his face, it was the first time that he had heard of the name. The future of my team may still have been well out of my control, but I felt in charge when I told him that he was staring right at the artist. My desire was so strong to help the Terriers to get out of trouble and the pat on the back from Roy only increased my eagerness to focus more fully on my mission in Manchester. It was only by accident that I ran into Roy Keane, but the fact that he responded so well and wished me all the best for the future made it feel like it was fate, or better still that I was getting help from above. The fact that he was only dressed in a plain T- shirt and jeans meant that he was harder to spot, making it easier to arrive at this conclusion. The reputation that he had built up along with his mileage for Manchester United meant that he was an ideal candidate to contribute to raising further awareness of our current crisis.

ROY KEANE

Despite turning down the chance to buy a ticket for the game, I had witnessed a stalemate on the T.V. surrounded by many neutrals in the pub. Ironically, I had witnessed a stalemate on the field as a result of trying to help one off it, referring to the financial deadlock back at Huddersfield. Having said this, the game was decided by penalties in favour of A.C.Milan to the delight of their traveling supporters. The team had clicked into gear to win the shoot-out after an exhausting contest.

Therefore, the jubilant sight of the Italian giants with the European Cup was one utter contrast with my team Huddersfield Town. Whilst A.C.Milan secured the highest honour in club football, my team was still clutching at straws in trying to simply stay alive. The star-studded Italians had arrived at their European destination, whereas the Terriers were still trying to swerve the demands of the creditors in the bumpy, rocky ride to possible safety. The journey was far from smooth and scenic amidst the continuous stalling and breaking down of negotiations, skidding and swerving round the deadlines, in and out of fresh hope and ideas to save the club. A.C.Milan did not have a care in the world as they were in a football nirvana, whereas the Blues were being driven up and down, backwards and forwards and from side to side in a financial reverse that was restless in nature.

However, despite the heartbreaking contrast between the clubs I never lost my focus amidst the noisy supporters, which may explain why I was so well rewarded before the night was over. This positive attitude along with being in the right place at the right time may explain why I was able to get so close to the A.C.Milan manager who had just won the Cup. However, even taking into account both of these factors, it still does not fully account for my surprise at being able to secure the signature of the Milan manager just minutes after such an extraordinary triumph. As I walked down the corridor at Old Trafford I was able to approach Carlos Angelotti, despite him being accompanied by security. This was totally different to the security that had confronted me at the McAlpine when I was sizing up the scale of the survival task in the early days. Back then I needed to convince the man on duty that my intentions were genuine as I gazed at the ground on that lonely Monday morning in the aftermath of relegation. However, to my amazement, here I was now walking along with the Italian chief with no questions being asked! As I touched his arm whilst congratulating him, I asked if he would sign my print of the Mc Alpine; I think I caught him at the right moment! Hence, without a word he wrote the boldest signature that I have ever seen in my life across the picture of the Stadium before disappearing out of sight. If only my old friend Simon Normington could have seen me now or any of my school friends for that matter!

ANGELLOTTI

Thus, I felt that I could not do much more to add to the high degree of satisfaction and accomplishment that I felt as a result of this experience. I did linger for quite a while, however, after the game, as I found it difficult to pull myself away from the crowds that were cheering the newly crowned European champions. The fact that there was a security barrier between us and the Milan giants, once again confirmed just how fortunate I had been in securing the manager's signature. The fact that you could only cheer or applaud the team as they got on the coach showed that my timing could not have been any better when I almost walked into the path of Angellotti. Yet, this was enough to generate such excitement to keep the fans in awe for quite a while. It certainly made sure that no-one noticed me with the pictures of the Mc Alpine Stadium in my hand as I felt like I was infiltrating the swollen ranks of the ecstatic Italians. The overwhelming sense of achievement that the fans were feeling made it easier for me to be incognito as an outsider, a Town fan in their midst.

Hence, the job was finished for A.C.Milan as it was indeed for me, as I was more than happy with my day's work in securing two massive autographs for the unfinished business back home. However, the only difference was that whereas the Milan maestros would be applauded and cheered amidst flashing, blinding photographs as they left, I slipped away unnoticed into the night.

Chapter 8: Feud for Thought.

"It's nice to meet you and to put a face to a name," was the response that I got when I met one of Town's favourite sons who had arranged to meet me for a chat.

Up until then he had never met me, but it was my alias name that had aroused his curiosity. With a pseudonym like goldenbrush, it would be hard not to scratch the surface of his curiosity as to what I looked like, but now Marcus Stewart had the chance to ask me any itchy questions that may have played on his mind as we came face to face.

It went without saying that I was pleased to see the one who had won the hearts of so many Town fans over the last few seasons at this brief meeting that had been arranged by his agent.

Having said this, how does a feud come into consideration at such an amicable meeting where Marcus was about to sign some prints for me? It would have been difficult to upset each other under such circumstances; in fact his willingness to co-operate with me was so evident by the fact that he asked Poomy (Mart Poom) the former Sunderland goalkeeper to take our picture

The Greatest Escape (In the History of Huddersfield Town F.C.)

together. The closest I came to any disagreement with the ace was when he said that he was sure that Sunderland would win the friendly at the McAlpine since they had a good side. However, even then I did not rise to the bait by saying that I thought that he was sadly mistaken. Since he was contributing to the much needed publicity by signing my prints I wanted to keep him sweet; hence it may have somewhat soured the occasion if I had contested his prediction in favour of a home win. Thus, although my encounter with Marcus went smoothly, it was what happened next that gave me food for thought, or 'feud for thought.'

MARCUS STEWART

I had already told the star striker that I had met Roy Keane at the European Cup Final in Manchester, and went on to tell him that he had signed a print for me.

I don't know if he figured out what was coming next, but I nevertheless made it clear that I would like to ask Mick McCarthy if he would sign the same picture as Roy had signed. I might have been a bit too hopeful in my thinking, but I reckoned that if I was successful then it would be a really good collector's item. If I could secure Mick's signature, the then Sunderland manager on the same print as what Roy had signed, then it would be a good collector's item given the well known fiery dispute that the pair had had. The fact that Mick and Roy had been involved in such a well documented, volatile bust-up whilst Mick was the manager of the Republic of Ireland was of much interest to me. I did not plan to open up old wounds between the two, but I simply saw this as an excellent way of generating further publicity for the survival cause. Due to the showdown that the pair had experienced during the World Cup for the Republic, the bringing together of the duo on my picture would seem like a reconciliatory gesture; one that was sure to bring about inescapable publicity. As I have already mentioned the results as regards the Great Escape were dependent on what happened on the field apart from the much needed inspiration from Jacko and Taff; to bring about the Greatest Escape ever, would be solely dependent on results off the field. Hence, to achieve what I call 'burying the hatchet' via the canvas as regards Mick McCarthy and Roy Keane would certainly be a result that could not easily be overlooked.

However, I should have listened to Marcus Stewart when he said that he would ask Mick to sign the print later. If I had done so it would have spared me from the somewhat embarrassing scene that was to follow.

The Greatest Escape (In the History of Huddersfield Town F.C.)

When the manager of the Black Cats passed in front of me I could not resist calling out his name in the hotel. When he turned round and asked what I wanted, I did not want to trick him in any way, which is why I asked him if he would sign a picture that Roy Keane had signed for me. The fact that he said "That's not very likely," as he made his way to the door, showed to me that the rift was still apparent, and that my attempt to heal it somewhat was in vain.

Having said this, although I did not get the result that I wanted I did have another chance or 'life' just like the cat, to add Mick to my growing collection. This was at the game a little later in the evening as he was standing on the touchline. At last, I was successful in adding his signature to one of my prints, having 'lost a life' in trying to involve Roy Keane.

MICK McCARTHY

J.B. Lockwood

Despite not having the two signatures on the same picture, it was ample reason to approach the newspaper once more in order to gain further coverage, in order to continue to lift the spirit of the club. Hence, I turned the feud, something that was negative into something that was positive in nature, as I tried to do my part in edging the club towards safety. The fact that one signature of Marcus Stewart among others helped me to sell one of my prints for £320 would no doubt have helped to raise the spirit more fully; the share that went to the Survival Trust would also have helped in a financial sense as we tried to keep the club afloat.

MCALPINE

However, despite this and other encouraging reports, were we on track for survival or were we in danger of being derailed in the near future? Find out in the penultimate chapter.

Chapter 9: Track to the Future?

Up until now there had been no shortage of recruits for the Survival Trust which had been fully committed to keeping Huddersfield Town alive. There was strong evidence of a united bond, a togetherness that had paid off in many respects. However, there were only scattered indications of light at the end of the tunnel; there was no real indication as to whether we would reach our destination. We were waiting for a signal to tell us that our efforts had not been in vain and that someone had come forward to rescue the Terriers from a collision course that would lead to disaster.

However, although there was no talk of surrendering or giving up on the idea of saving the Blues, there was only so much that the fans could do to ease the situation; it was more a case of putting the brakes on the financial slide as we played for even more time. But how much time was left? Where would the breakthrough come from to release the club from its captive condition? How long could we keep the momentum going without running out of steam? Given the fact that the final whistle could soon be blown on the blue and white outfit, did not make for a comfortable journey; rather the restlessness was apparent due to the fact that if the whistle was blown then there would be no extra time to settle the issue.

I thought about the times that I had travelled to see my team and the many hours that had been spent in following the Terriers and the sacrifices that I had made as a result, hoping that there would be more good times to come.

I recall on one occasion going down to Bournemouth when we were in the old Fourth Division, at a time when the club was in one of its darker periods, lingering in the wrong half of the table. This, however, did not stop me from traveling all night to see the Town on the south coast to take on the Cherries.

I don't remember how the game turned out but I do remember being pushed into the icy sea at about eight o' clock in the morning. I recall my socks and shoes being wet through for hours; in fact I don't think they actually dried out fully that day. Moreover, if I am not mistaken, I think that the team leaked a few goals to add to dampen my spirit more fully. Having said that at least they did not have to wait until they arrived back in Yorkshire to get a change of clothing!

However, looking back, it was good fun and at least we knew that we still had a team to support even if we had to apply for re-election. This was when the side that finished bottom of the Football League had to apply for permission to be officially reinstated.

Many fans, no doubt, have kept programs and memorabilia and have kept a track on how the football club has performed over the years.

However, the one vital statistic that the fans needed to hear, was that a consortium or a new owner was to take over Huddersfield Town to bring about a new era. In the absence of such an announcement, the breathtaking reality was that the club would disappear leaving everyone with a date that could not be forgotten for the wrong reason.

However, at the end of May 2003, when the High Court in Leeds granted an extra three months to settle the issues that were putting our survival in jeopardy, it was good news for the consortium headed by Terry Fisher. It meant that the club was still on track for a possible rescue bid, despite being still in administration in the hands of Begbies Traynor. I for one was grateful for any signal to suggest that the club was heading in the right direction, so this was a positive announcement in the long and exhausting saga.

The fact that the Survival Trust publicly declared that they had raised £120,000 with the purpose of keeping Huddersfield Town alive was also a timely boost to add to the newfound momentum and optimism, as a result of the High Court's decision.

Having said this, the ride to possible safety would never be smooth. Despite good, ongoing support and backing from the consortium, the P.F.A. according to Terry Fisher were being intransigent. It was not just the other members of the consortium, including Ken Davy, Martin Byrne and the Norweigan, Vidar Forsdalt that were experiencing a rocky ride; it was also the many thousands of fans that were being thrown around on this restless journey.

The Greatest Escape (In the History of Huddersfield Town F.C.)

One of the songs that has been around, and sung by the fans for many years is a revised version of Those Were the Days My Friend; a song made popular by Mary Hopkins in the sixties. Among the lyrics are the words…we lived the life we choose; we'd fight and never lose, for we were young and sure to have our way… These words that Simon and I used to sing suggest an indestructible spirit and optimism based on the rich heritage and tradition that belong to the proud club. Although it was true that we were not having things our own way, nevertheless we were determined to keep the unbreakable spirit that still echoes through the years, right down to the great Herbert Chapman.

The fact that Jacko had decided to 'come home' despite brief uncertainty and speculation as regards his future, helped the spirit of optimism. This kept us on course for the following season as regards matters on the pitch which helped to promote more passion as regards the raging battle off it.

Fascinatingly enough, the return of the 'King' in the person of Peter Jackson was mirrored by the epic tale of The Lord of the Rings and the Return of the King which was dominating cinemas everywhere. The fact that another Peter Jackson had already directed this compelling saga helped me to forge a strong link between the two tales that were both drawing national attention.

In the fantasy adventure the king Aragon had been containing or rejecting evil forces on his return to Mordor, amidst the ever-present threat of Sauron. On the other hand, although he had not been involved in such drama, as far as I am aware, Jacko had been resisting offers and attention from other clubs. Hence, despite not being involved in a life or death issue his focus and passion for the Terriers had remained undiminished. The talk of his possible return only helped the positive spirit that was prevalent for the most part; it did no harm at all, and it did not distract in any way the track for the future. The biggest obstacle was to make sure that the creditors were satisfied with the developments off the field rather than some evil predator. It was not the hurling, swirling clouds of evil menace that stood in the way of Jacko's return, but it was nevertheless the oppressive race against time to find an agreement with the debtors that was threatening to rob us of strength and moisture in the fight for continued existence. Although he may have a similar passion and resolve to the mythical figure in the saga, unlike the king in the epic he could do nothing to reverse the financial chasm that was still threatening swallow us up; there was still a possibility of the wheels coming off our assault and the inevitability of plunging into oblivion as the burning issue of survival continued to rage.

Despite this sobering fact, whilst the nation were waiting to see if Aragon the king would answer the call of his heritage and take up his kingship, our primary concern was to see if Peter Jackson would answer the question of his royal role. If the issue was answered to satisfaction it would only have a settling influence on the campaign; it could only give added momentum to our journey which would hopefully end in our intended destination. His very presence and limited involvement could only increase our chances of completing a successful journey and in bringing about the Greatest Escape that the club had known. Despite being thrown from side to side as it were Terry Fisher was determined to retain his balance and composure. Although the Terriers were not allowed any voting rights in the Football League, he nevertheless did not want to be coerced into overspending to the point where the pot was empty as regards future investment. He said that 'we need to draw lines in the sand that cannot be crossed', expressing his resolve not to be swayed by pressure from inside or outside sources.

Thus the leadership qualities that helped to ensure the Great Escape were still in evidence for a potential Escape of a far greater magnitude. This may have accounted in some measure for the positive spirit that was shown by Paul Scott who added further stability to the club by signing a new one year contract; a timely boost for us since he had been voted the Player of the Year for the reserves the season which had just ended.

This feeling of stability, however, was only short-lived since the club was once again rocked by a demand for a cash injection for £50,000, to cover trading costs. Among these costs was a figure for £2,500 which had to be paid to the Football Association as a penalty for six bookings that had been picked up at Port Vale on the last day of the season which was full of torment. Little did we realise just how these bookings would come to haunt us at a future date, despite the fact that they went largely unnoticed on the day. Thankfully, due to the generous contributions from the fans, the Survival Trust was able to comply with this demand.

There was still light at the end of the tunnel, nevertheless, until we were rocked once more with the shuddering news that Terry Fisher had withdrawn his support from the consortium. Knowing that we would miss his undoubted passion and funding, it seemed like we had been plunged into a temporary darkness.

Despite the subdued feeling of the loss of Terry, Martyn Byrne confirmed his solid, whole hearted intention to save the club from liquidation in an attempt to once more lift the spirit; he was adamant that the sustained efforts would not grind to a halt. He was, like many others, determined to build on the financial platform that we had.

The loss of balance had been felt, however, in this setback and was felt even more so with the uncertainty over the future of Martin Smith. Although last season's top striker was considering a new two year deal he was owed a considerable sum in unpaid wages; hence the stalling continued amidst fresh optimism that Jacko could once more restore pride and dignity to the club which had fallen from grace in such a short time. We were still being pushed from side to side in an attempt to maintain a steady momentum.

This momentum was made even harder to achieve by the £30,000 police bill for maintaining order at the matches. Despite a limited amount of help with League and Cup matches, they insisted on being paid for friendly matches which is why some had to be cancelled; the games against local rivals Bradford City and Halifax Town were two fixtures that had to be abandoned. This was indicative of the complicated scenario and the entangled financial web that had been spun around the blue and white outfit. Thus, the ongoing commitment from everyone was a factor in trying to promote continuity and an eventual release.

Chapter 10: The Greatest Escape.

On the 24 July a bolt came out of the blue for the Blues. Ken Davy, the Giants supremo, was quoted as making an offer of £1.4 million pounds to settle the unpaid wages to keep the rescue mission on track. If the players accepted the offer then it would be the removal of a big obstacle to further progress; in other words it would pave the way for the Greatest Escape ever known to anyone, associated with the Terriers.

The signs were promising that an agreement could be reached to satisfy the issue of unpaid wages for the players. This would be a big breakthrough in turning things around; step in the right direction in achieving the right kind of ASBO a safe, blue outfit, as opposed to a sorry one. The safety would mean far more that it did in the Great Escape. Without being dismissive of the tremendous work and passion that went into achieving such an outcome, the Greatest Escape would signify much more than avoiding relegation to a lower division; it would mean 'cheating' the death of an illustrious football club.

The Greatest Escape (In the History of Huddersfield Town F.C.)

Whilst waiting for news to filter through as regards Ken Davy's solid offer, he showed no sign of weakness by appointing Andrew Watson as Chief Executive to give the club more stability.

There was nothing elementary about his new role with Town still in a state of financial limbo; to the contrary he was facing a complicated scenario on the back of a prolonged fight for our very existence.

The fact that he had supported the Terriers from childhood would no doubt help his commitment in these troubled and uncertain times. He had seen Town do things the hard way which would qualify him not only for the present struggle, but also during the possible takeover which would be anything but smooth. It did not take much power of deduction to realise that there would be an aftermath of adjustment and organization to take things forward should the Greatest Escape become a reality.

Therefore, when news filtered through that settlement of unpaid wages had been reached it was confirmation of the breakthrough that everyone was waiting for in this period of further limbo. It was true to say that it was a massive step in taking the blues away, whilst trying to make sure that the BLUES remained.

Hence, when Ken Davy made it clear that a takeover deal would be concluded it helped to lift the spirit more fully, as it meant that any lingering anxieties about the immediate future of the Terriers should soon be removed. The fact that Ken said that he was 95% sure of a settlement being reached would surely inspire hope, relief and a sense of freedom to many who had felt trapped during the dark period of administration.

The future was looking a whole lot brighter as we were on the verge of an historical announcement; in fact, according to Mr. Davy it was only a matter of time before the technicalities would be removed paving the way for the club's salvation. This was not like waiting for an announcement over whether a game should be played or not, or finding out who was in the team and who was injured or the fixtures for a new season; this was a case of waiting to hear the confirmation that our team was safe from the threat of folding as a football club. The implications of the anticipated announcement were far, far, greater that anything that anyone had known before in the club's illustrious history.

Hence, on 31st July, 2003 after an announcement from Ken Davy in the Huddersfield Examiner I am sure that everyone associated with the club felt a massive relief. This was the day that we were told that Huddersfield Town F.C. was SAVED!

Despite having been only eight days from closure with debts of around £20 million pounds, we had experienced the Greatest Escape when the Terriers had been rescued from liquidation.

Thus whilst Chelsea had brought their summer spending to £52 million pounds, our blue and white outfit was content with the lifeline that had been given us after exhausting months of talks, discussions and having been plagued by sheer uncertainty over our future.

Having said this, a team like Chelsea had plenty of scope to experiment with new players in a seemingly endless financial budget, whereas this was not the case with the Terriers; there was little or no margin for mistakes as our world turned Davy blue.

The Greatest Escape (In the History of Huddersfield Town F.C.)

Although we were overjoyed with the unlikely outcome of Town's future, there were still restraints and conditions that had to be met, due to the casualties that had arisen. One of these involved the 517 bondholders that had paid £375,661 for season tickets for the next four years. Hence, it was nice to see that their unrivalled commitment as fans to the cause did not go unnoticed as Ken Davy wrote to each and every one of them as a token of his indebtedness. What a contrast this attitude was to some that I used to see climbing over the gates at the old Leeds Road ground instead of paying at the turnstiles. This was a time when Simon and I used to sway backwards and forwards in the Cowshed having nothing to worry about, apart from perhaps our bus fare home. At that time I had no idea just how much trouble the club would end up in; hardship then was queuing for a pie and walking into Town at the end of the game.

In addition to trying to make amends to the bondholders who lost out financially, there was the need for a rallying call from Ken with regard to ongoing support and commitment from business and commerce in the community.

Therefore, despite having reached the daylight at the end of the tunnel, this conditional freedom was granted only after every single element of the takeover had been debated and agreed.

Ken Davy personally told me that when he came forward with his offer to rescue the club that the hand of the 'clock' was at one minute to midnight. Hence without his timely intervention there would have been no Huddersfield Town. If he had let the three deadlines go which had been set by the administrators, without any solid offer, then the club would have disappeared; thankfully he acted just in time. I am at total loss as to who you would have blamed if the club had gone into liquidation, but someone would have been made a scapegoat in the guilt –ridden enquiry that would surely have followed. There would have been no end to the shifting of blame as enquiry upon enquiry would have drawn out a real sense of anger, bitterness and resentment. It would have been so difficult to deal with and to move on. Thankfully, this punishing, bitter enquiry was averted at the last minute,by extremely good timing from the man in charge of the Giants. As our world turned Davy blue, it saved us from either switching to another club or going shopping on a Saturday afternoon, perhaps with someone who had no interest in football. Thankfuliy we don't have to dwell on such an imagined scenario which would have tormented true fans for many years to come.

KEN DAVY

The Greatest Escape (In the History of Huddersfield Town F.C.)

However, although it can be said that Ken Davy saved the Terriers, this brings me to a crucial point: I do believe that the fans and others deserve some credit. In other words if the supporters had shown little passion and commitment especially in the early days of administration would there still have been a club to save? By Ken. Moreover, if there had not been much interest by the fans to keep the Terriers alive, why would the main creditors such as Barry Rubery wish to write off so much debt? Without the passion, desire and sacrifices in raising awareness of the situation then it would have been difficult to shift such a massive debt that the club owed. I think it very unlikely that Ken would have wanted to be involved with debts of anything like £20 million pounds even if he could have taken it on; hence the Survival Trust and the fans in general helped to reduce the arrears to the point where a realistic offer could be made by the supremo to bring about the Greatest Escape.

IT WAS A SMALL STEP FOR KEN DAVY, BUT A GIANT LEAP FOR THE BLUE AND WHITE OF MANKIND.

In conclusion, I have to say that I have not met my old school friend Simon Normington for many years now. I sometimes wonder if I will bump into him when I am in the queue for a cup of coffee. (By the way, I still cannot be guaranteed a lid for my cup!) I feel that our paths have crossed however, without having seen each other. I am sure that he was just as relieved with the life-saving contribution from Ken Davy as I was, not to mention the relief of the thousands of fans who have been associated with the Terriers. I am sure that there will be thrilling times ahead in the highs and lows that are to come for the club, but I cannot imagine anything to eclipse the importance and drama and joy of the Greatest Escape in the history of Huddersfield Town.

Printed in Great Britain
by Amazon